Meerkats

For Kids

Amazing Animal Books for Young Readers

by Lisa Barry

Mendon Cottage Books

JD-Biz Publishing

Download Free Books!

http://MendonCottageBooks.com

Read More Amazing Animal Books

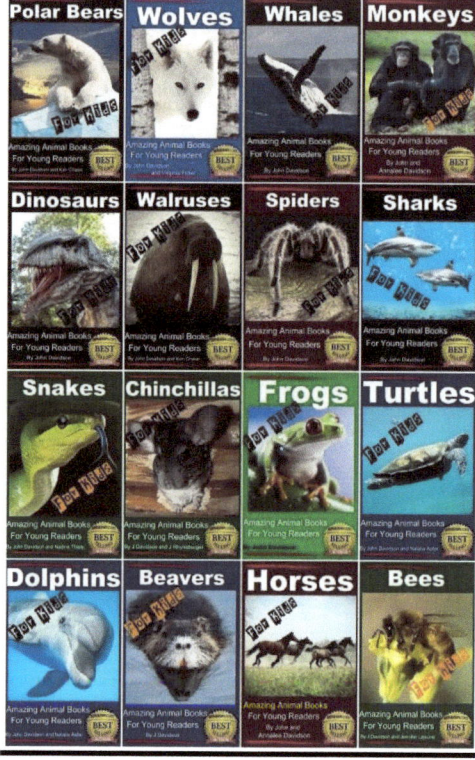

Purchase at Amazon.com

Download Free Books!

http://MendonCottageBooks.com

Table of Contents

Meerkat Facts

- Meerkats are mammals. This means that they breathe with lungs like humans.
- Meerkats live in large groups. People refer to these groups as a mob, gang or clan.
- Meerkats are omnivores. This means they eat meat and vegetables.
- Meerkats are also known as Suricate or Suricata Suricata. The word means "Lake Cat" but Meerkats are not related to cats at all.
- They belong to the mongoose family.

- In the wild they live for 6 - 8 years.
- A baby meerkat is called a pup.

What do Meerkats Look Like?

- Meerkats are small. On average they are 10 inches. This is about the same height as a big cat.
- They weigh about 1.6lb which is less than a bag of sugar.
- The meerkats body is slim with long arms and short legs.
- They have long tails that are thin with a pointed end. They use their tails to balance when they stand upright and to help them to communicate.
- The meerkats face has a pointy nose with black patches around the eyes. These are different on each meerkat and enables them identify each other.

- They have small ears that they can put close to the ground when looking and listening for food. They are able to close their ears which is a very unusual skill. They do this to keep the soil out of their ears when they are digging.
- They have claws to help them dig the soil.
- They have 4 digits on each hand and foot.
- They have fawn/sandy coloured fur with stripes on their back.
- They have a balder patch on their stomachs that help them to take in and keep the heat in when it gets cold.

Where Do Meerkats Live

Meerkats live in desert areas. Deserts are hot and dry places but they can also get very cold. They are very harsh places to live and for any animal to survive there they must be specially equipped to handle the conditions.

Examples of other animals that live in the desert are;

- Ostrich
- Roadrunner
- Lizard
- Toad
- Black Widow Spider (very poisonous)
- Hyena
- Gecko
- Rattlesnake
- Cobra

Meerkats can be found in the deserts of Angola, South Africa, Nambia and Botswana. All of these places are on the southern part of the African continent.

The heat in the summer may seem extreme to us. It can be as high as 158(f) / 70 (c) It gets a lots cooler in the nights and the winter. The temperature can drop to 14 (f) or -10 (c).The meerkats have to be adaptable to these very different conditions.

The rain in the desert is minimal. Although there is little surface water there is water under the soil that the meerkat can get to. It rains about 12 inches over the whole year but that is nearly always in the winter. Meerkats hate the rain.

The Meerkat Home

Meerkats make themselves their home by digging a series of complicated tunnels underground. They have many different entrances. These are called burrows. They sleep in these all night and only leave in the day to hunt for food. These burrows also have mounds. These mounds are created by the excess piles of dirt created when digging the tunnels. However they serve a double purpose, these offer a good vantage point for the meerkats to stand and survey the land looking for danger. They also have separate sleeping chambers. The reason they make it so complicated is to help protect them selves by giving them lots of hiding options.

Meerkats will sometimes have to move and build a whole new burrow. This is a complicated and long process and therefore they will only do it if it is absolutely necessary. Reasons that meerkats may have to move are;

- A rival gang taking over the territory.
- Food sources running out.

Sometimes other animals live in the burrow with the meerkats. These are likely to be either yellow mongooses or a ground squirrels. When this occurs they live side by side with no conflict. They do not interfere with each other or each others food supply. It is not always that peaceful when the meerkats find they are sharing a home with a snake!

What Do Meerkats Eat?

Meerkats do not have any excess body fat. This means that they do not store any of food in their bodies. They therefore must eat regularly through out the day. As they have to also search for their food, a meerkats day is primarily taken up by food.

Most of the meerkat diet is made up of insects. They also eat;

- Snakes
- Scorpions
- Spiders
- Eggs
- Plants
- Elephant Shrews

Some of their food is very poisonous but the meerkat body is prepared for this. It has a special immunity to many strong types of venom. This means that if they get stung by a spider or a scorpion, they won't get hurt as much as we would. It is one of the ways that the meerkat can survive in the harsh desert. Without this immunity they would struggle to find all the food they need. They would also be more venerable themselves.

They find their food by foraging. This means they search and dig the ground. This process involves a high level of team work. Meerkats are amazing diggers. They use their claws to dig the dry desert soil. They will always work together in their group.

When foraging at least one member is given the task of being sentry. This role is only temporary and they all take it in turns. The sentry is responsible for the safety of the whole group by watching for predators (animals that want to eat the meerkats). When they are safe the sentry will keep the group informed of this by making peeping sounds. When there is danger they whistle or bark very loudly. There will always be at least one sentry on guard, even if the other meerkats are resting in the open or playing, it is essential they have a look out so they can work as a group to avoid danger. When the sentry signals that that there is danger, they all run as quickly a possible under cover, ideally into their burrows. This is why they prefer to forage for food close to their home. When food is scarce and they have to go further afield it is much more risky. Meerkats will not even leave their underground home in the morning, without the signal from the sentry that the outside is free from predators.

Baby meerkats do not join the forage. They have to wait till they are at least a month old. When they are learning how to forage they follow an experienced, older meerkat who is the "pup tutor."

What Animals Eat Meerkats?

- Martial Eagle – with a wing spa of 6 inches they will snatch and eat an adult meerkat.

- Smaller birds of prey will go for the easier option and try to take the babies. Simply because they are lighter to carry.

- Jackal – for this animal the meerkat is a valued food source.

- Cobras – they will not be able to strike an adult because they are too agile. They can however, if given a chance, strike kill and eat the young meerkats.

The Meerkat Mob

Meerkats are very social little animals and have complicated relationships. They live in groups of up to 30 meerkats. They are very affectionate to each other and will groom and stroke each other; they even do this as a loving way to greet one another if they haven't seen each other for some time.

There is always an alpha pair; a male and female meerkat who are in charge of the rest of the group. They are often the mom and dad to most of the members. To show they are in charge they will often scent mark (urinate on) the others and then they will have to stroke the alpha back, as if to say thank you!

Meerkats sleep, forage and eat but they also play. Even the adult meerkats do. They have been observed taking part in wrestling matches so they clearly have a sense of fun. They have also been observed playing with objects like human children play with toys. Even when they are having fun they still have a sentry on guard to watch over the group and keep them safe

Rival mobs can cause a big threat to meerkat groups. The main reason that the different groups may fight is because of space. They may fight over territory because the land is their food source. When a fight is on the cards they start to jump and puff up their fur. This is to make them selves look bigger. This is called "mobbing." This won't always result in a fight, sometimes one group decides that the others look too strong and simply leave the territory. When they do fight it can be 3 against one at times. They jump on each others back and bite and scratch. It is the alpha males who decides who has won. If they assess the decision and decide that they have lost too many meerkats or the members are too injured then he calls the group to retreat.

Another time that meerkats may fight is if there is a lone or small group of meerkats looking to either have babies with some of the females in the mob or to join the group themselves. The decision on if they are allowed to join or not will be the result of the "mobbing."

Meerkats mobs will break down if;

1. A predator attacks and kills or seriously injures a large part of the group or specifically the alpha pair.
2. The alpha pair not being able to have any more babies.
3. Weather – if there is no rain for a particularly long time this is called a drought. In the desert, which is a very dry place anyway, this can have a devastating affect on the land and creatures that live there. A drought can cause the meerkat mob to die of thirst or starvation. Also if there is rain in the summer, they need to get the young babies to higher ground in case the burrows flood. This makes them vulnerable to predators.
4. If there is a disease outbreak or illness that kills meerkats. They are prone to rabies.

5. If a group becomes too big, they will have to look for food further from their burrow. When danger is signalled and they have to run for cover, the meerkats who are far away (this is never the alpha pair), will end up finding closer holes to hide in. If this continues for a long time then they may naturally end up forming a separate group.

The Meerkat Family

Meerkats can have babies any time of the year. The female meerkats are pregnant for 11 weeks. Each litter (pregnancy) usually has about 4-5 pups.

The Meerkat mob look after each other and each of them take some responsibility for taking care of the young. The females that have never had babies can make milk and feed the baby meerkats.

The babies will have babysitters. They have to be able to protect the little ones in case there is danger and they sometimes have to die to ensure their safety. If there is any sign of danger the babysitter is responsible for getting them underground in their burrow. However, sometimes they may be too far away, or the danger may be in between them and the burrow. In these cases the babysitter will get the babies to lie down and then lie on top of them.

It is up to the alpha pair who is allowed to have babies within the group. Often these meerkats in charge will kill any babies that other meerkats in the mob have, unless they have allowed it. This will usually result in the mother of the killed babies being evicted from the mob. New mobs may be made when these evicted females find a lone male meerkat. They can start their own group and be the alpha pair.

Sometimes the female alpha will die and an older daughter takes over the alpha role. When this happens they will find lone males for the new top girl to have babies with so that they she doesn't have to have babies with any male meerkat that is her brother.

Meerkats Life Cycle

Stages of a Meerkats Growth	Age
The babies are born underground. They are blind and deaf when they are born. They have hair but not full fur.	0
They open their eyes and can see	10 – 14 weeks
They open their ears and can hear	15 days
They come out of the burrow. They stay with the babysitter by the entrance to the burrow.	21 days
They start to forage, with the guidance of the pup tutor.	28 days
They stop drinking milk altogether and start eating the same as the adult meerkats. This is called weaning and all baby animals go through this process, including humans.	49 – 63 days
Meerkats continue to learn by watching the others in the mob. From taking the sting out of a scorpion to learning to listen for movement underground (this signals moving food). They first watch their elders do it and then they are physically taught these skills by the pup tutor. This is a bit like meerkat school.	3 weeks – 1 year.
Meerkats are fully adult and able to have babies. They are expected to start to take on some of the important roles such as babysitter and sentry.	1 year

Although these roles are usually and more often taken by the older more experience in the group. They are also to forage independently. No role is forced upon the meerkat before they are ready though, they have a lot of support from their tutor and other meerkats in the group to ensure they are confident. In many cases the stakes can be life or death so it is important each meerkat is competent in their roles.	
Meerkats die.	6 – 8 years old in the wild Up to 15 years in captivity.

How do meerkats speak to each other?

Meerkats make a variety of noises, they bark, they growl, they trill and chirrup.

The most important reason that meerkats need an effective way to communicate is to warn each other of predators. The job of foraging involves the meerkat looking and listening closely at the ground as they are digging, therefore the role of the lookout (the sentry), it vital for the groups safety.

The job is not a simple one though; they do not just have to simply call out when there is danger. They have to signify exactly what the danger is, this enables the mob to act in the best way to keep themselves safe.

The meerkat sentry has to make a very specific call to notify the mob of birds of prey, for example eagles. They make 3 different types of calls to signify how close the danger is.

The sentry has a completely different call for animals that could pose a threat on the ground like cobras. Again they make 3 different types of calls to signify how close the danger is.

This means that they have a total of 6 different warning calls; each one means that the rest of the meerkat mob reacts in a different way to prepare for possible danger. An example of this is if a call went out to say that an eagle was very close and the mob was in imminent danger. They may not have enough time to get to their burrows, so they have to take action by crouching down low to avoid being spotted.

A Day in the Life of a Meerkat.

- Wake up early – as soon as the sun rises.
- Check that the area is safe. This is the job of the sentry. The same sentry that was on duty in the night as they went into the burrow, will be on duty first thing in the morning and will therefore be the first meerkat out of the burrow in the morning.
- A little time resting in the sun and slowly waking up is allowed. This does serve a purpose though. As their little bodies have had to endure the cold of the desert night, this gives them the opportunity to warm up. Their bare bellies are like solar panels, giving them energy for the day of foraging ahead. The young will use this time to play and meerkats of all ages will groom each other.
- When they start to feel hungry they will start the hunt for food. The alpha decides where they should forage.
- They will stop for rest periods throughout the day. These periods will be longer when it is summer as the day is longer and the heat is hotter.
- They return to their burrows main entrance just before the sunsets and just like in the morning, they have a relaxing period. Once again they play and groom each other. This is also the time they make any repairs or improvements on their burrow.
- They retreat to their burrow as the sun sets, one by one. The sentry being the last. This meerkat will be the first out in the morning.

Meerkat relatives

Meerkats belong to the mongoose family. There are 35 different types of mongoose but most are not social like the meerkat. Its close, sociable relatives are;

- The bandid
- The Kousi Mansi

- Dwarf mongoose.

Most other types of mongoose are nocturnal. This means they sleep in the day and they hunt at night. Meerkats are different though because they always spend the night time in their burrows and hunt in the day.

Meerkats in Captivity

When a meerkat mob is in captivity, most probably a zoo environment, their life is potentially different. They have no predators, an abundance of food and they don't have the space to forage further and therefore move burrows or splinter off into different groups. The result of this is that their senses become dulled, they loose their innate ability to communicate as well as they would in the wild because it is not necessary for survival. They obviously do well in captivity as they have more babies and live longer.

Did you know?

- In African folklore the meerkat protects villagers from the werewolf (Moon Devil). They call the meerkat the Sun Angel.

- A meerkat is so good at digging, they can dig their own body weight in soil in less that a minuet. Can you imagine having to dig the same amount of soil as you weigh – with your hands? It would probably take a lot longer than a minuet. That is one of the reasons humans are not made to live in the desert!

- When new meerkats are born or venture out of the burrow for the first time, some of the adolescent pups, the equivalent to human teenagers, may act silly. This is to try to get more attention than the new babies.

- Meerkats urinate in their own bedroom chambers. This may sound quite horrible to us humans but, like many things the meerkat does, is for safety. A meerkat would not venture out alone at night to go to the toilet so the solution is obvious! Also they rely on urine as a scent and it is there way to mark their territory.

- There are certain types of beetles the meerkats do not eat. They live in the burrows with them. It is believed that the meerkats will leave these because they eat the meerkat poo!

Could I Have a Meerkat As a pet?

Question: Meerkats love to live in groups, why wouldn't they love to live in a human house hold?

Answer: Meerkats are group animals but they have very specific rules that a humans household won't follow. This will cause the meerkat to be anxious and they may then be destructive in your house.

Question: Meerkats eat food that I can buy in a pet store so can I give them all the food they need?

Answer: It is not just the food itself that a meerkat needs. They need to forage and no amount of shop bought bugs will stop them from digging up your carpet.

Question: Will meerkats smell in my house?

Answer: Meerkats urinate to scent an area, much like dogs. You will not be able to train a meerkat not to do it though. They will cause an extremely unpleasant smell in your house.

Question: As they are social creatures will they enjoy being in a busy house and meeting new people who come?

Answer: Social animals are not the same as social humans. Meerkats will get very nervous with newcomers which will result in extreme aggression.

Conclusion: Meerkats **DO NOT** make good pets!

Read More Amazing Animal Books

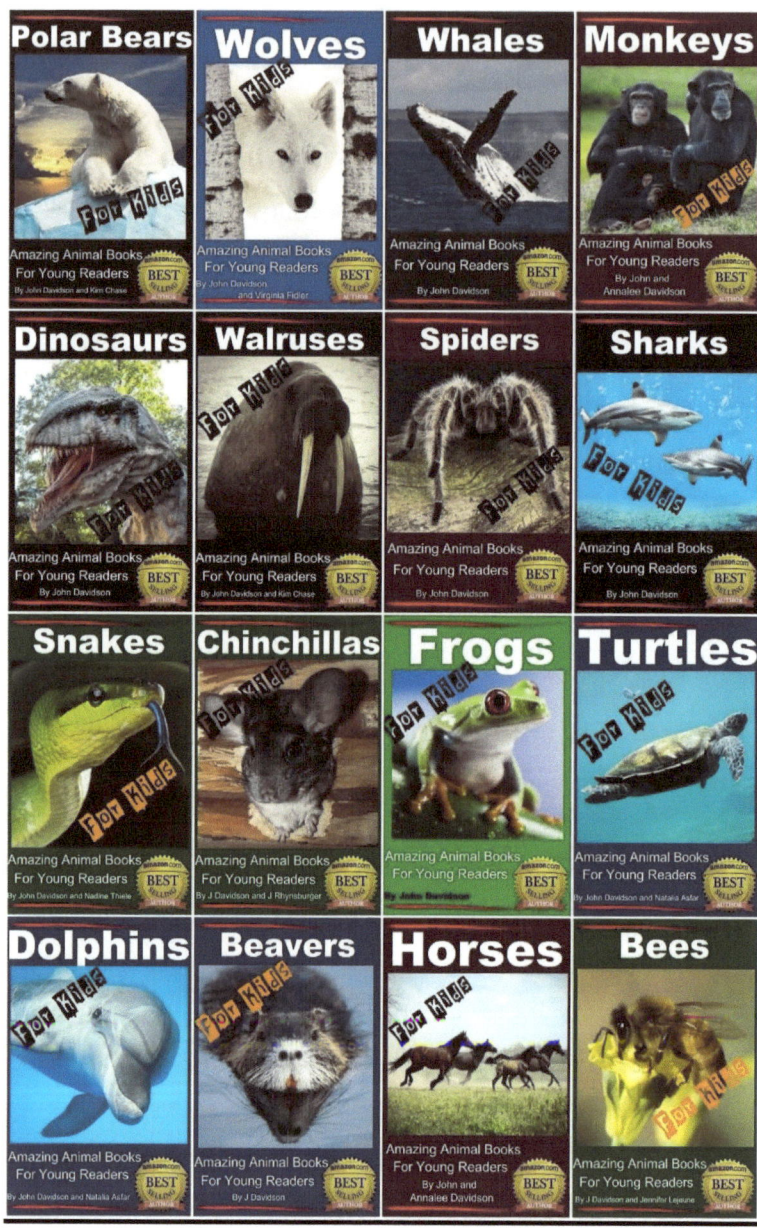

Purchase at Amazon.com

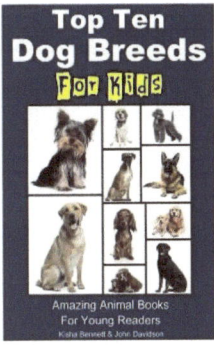

Top Ten Dog Breeds For Kids

Amazing Animal Books For Young Readers
Kisha Bennett & John Davidson

German Shepherds

Dog Books for Kids
K. Bennett

Bulldogs

Dog Books for Kids
K. Bennett

Dachshund

Dog Books for Kids
K. Bennett

Poodles

Dog Books for Kids
K. Bennett

Labrador Retrievers

Dog Books for Kids
K. Bennett

Rottweilers

Dog Books for Kids
K. Bennett

Boxers

Dog Books for Kids
K. Bennett

Golden Retrievers

Dog Books for Kids
K. Bennett

Puppies

Dog Books For Kids

Amazing Animal Books
By John Davidson

Beagles

Dog Books for Kids
K. Bennett

Yorkshire Terriers

Dog Books for Kids
K. Bennett

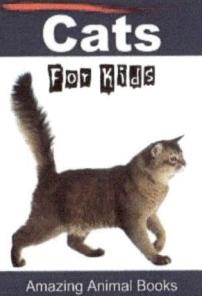

Dogs
Top Ten Dog Breeds For Kids

Amazing Animal Books For Young Readers
Zahra Jazeel & John Davidson

Cats For Kids

Amazing Animal Books For Young Readers
K. Bennett & John Davidson

Foxes For Kids

Amazing Animal Books For Young Readers
Zahra Jazeel & John Davidson

Wolves For Kids

Amazing Animal Books For Young Readers
By John Davidson and Virginia Fidler

Our books are available at

1. Amazon.com

2. Barnes and Noble

3. Itunes

4. Kobo

5. Smashwords

6. Google Play Books

Download Free Books!

http://MendonCottageBooks.com

Publisher

JD-Biz Corp

P O Box 374

Mendon, Utah 84325

http://www.jd-biz.com/

Mendon Cottage Books

P O Box 374, Mendon Utah 84325

www.ingramcontent.com/pod-product-compliance
Lightning Source LLC
Chambersburg PA
CBHW050859290526
45792CB00002B/664